MznLnx

Missing Links Exam Preps

Exam Prep for

Project Managment A Managerial Approach

Meredith & Mantel, Jr., 6th Edition

The MznLnx Exam Prep is your link from the texbook and lecture to your exams.
The MznLnx Exam Preps are unauthorized and comprehensive reviews of your textbooks.

All material provided by MznLnx and Rico Publications (c) 2010
Textbook publishers and textbook authors do not particpate in or contribute to these reviews.

MznLnx

Rico Publications

Exam Prep for Project Managment A Managerial Approach
6th Edition
Meredith & Mantel, Jr.

Publisher: Raymond Houge
Assistant Editor: Michael Rouger
Text and Cover Designer: Lisa Buckner
Marketing Manager: Sara Swagger
Project Manager, Editorial Production: Jerry Emerson
Art Director: Vernon Lowerui

Product Manager: Dave Mason
Editorial Asitant: Rachel Guzmanji
Pedagogy: Debra Long
Cover Image: Jim Reed/Getty Images
Text and Cover Printer: City Printing, Inc.
Compositor: Media Mix, Inc.

(c) 2010 Rico Publications
ALL RIGHTS RESERVED. No part of this work covered by the copyright may be reproduced or used in any form or by an means--graphic, electronic, or mechanical, including photocopying, recording, taping, Web distribution, information storage, and retrieval systems, or in any other manner--without the written permission of the publisher.

Printed in the United States
ISBN:

For more information about our products, contact us at:
Dave.Mason@RicoPublications.com

For permission to use material from this text or product, submit a request online to:
Dave.Mason@RicoPublications.com

Contents

CHAPTER 1
Projects in Contemporary Organizations — 1

CHAPTER 2
Strategic Management and Project Selection — 4

CHAPTER 3
The Project Manager — 10

CHAPTER 4
Project Organization — 15

CHAPTER 5
Project Planning — 18

CHAPTER 6
Conflict and Negotiation — 23

CHAPTER 7
Budgeting and Cost Estimation — 25

CHAPTER 8
Scheduling — 31

CHAPTER 9
Resource Allocation — 37

CHAPTER 10
Monitoring and Information Systems — 43

CHAPTER 11
Project Control — 48

CHAPTER 12
Project Auditing — 53

CHAPTER 13
Project Termination — 55

ANSWER KEY — 57

TO THE STUDENT

COMPREHENSIVE

The *MznLnx* Exam Prep series is designed to help you pass your exams. Editors at MznLnx review your textbooks and then prepare these practice exams to help you master the textbook material. Unlike study guides, workbooks, and practice tests provided by the texbook publisher and textbook authors, *MznLnx* gives you **all** of the material in each chapter in exam form, not just samples, so you can be sure to nail your exam.

MECHANICAL

The MznLnx Exam Prep series creates exams that will help you learn the subject matter as well as test you on your understanding. Each question is designed to help you master the concept. Just working through the exams, you gain an understanding of the subject--its a simple mechanical process that produces success.

INTEGRATED STUDY GUIDE AND REVIEW

MznLnx is not just a set of exams designed to test you, its also a comprehensive review of the subject content. Each exam question is also a review of the concept, making sure that you will get the answer correct without having to go to other sources of material. You learn as you go! Its the easiest way to pass an exam.

HUMOR

Studying can be tedious and dry. MznLnx's instructional design includes moderate humor within the exam questions on occassion, to break the tedium and revitalize the brain

Chapter 1. Projects in Contemporary Organizations

1. _____ in organizations and public policy is both the organizational process of creating and maintaining a plan; and the psychological process of thinking about the activities required to create a desired goal on some scale. As such, it is a fundamental property of intelligent behavior. This thought process is essential to the creation and refinement of a plan, or integration of it with other plans, that is, it combines forecasting of developments with the preparation of scenarios of how to react to them.

   a. Back-end database
   b. 68-95-99.7 rule
   c. 8.3 filename
   d. Planning

2. _____ is the discipline of planning, organizing and managing resources to bring about the successful completion of specific project goals and objectives.

   A project is a finite endeavor--having specific start and completion dates--undertaken to meet particular goals and objectives, usually to bring about beneficial change or added value. This finite characteristic of projects stands in contrast to processes, or operations--which is repetitive, permanent or semi-permanent functional work to produce products or services.

   a. Risk register
   b. Logical framework approach
   c. SMART
   d. Project management

3. _____ is a business management strategy, initially implemented by Motorola, that today enjoys widespread application in many sectors of industry.

   _____ seeks to improve the quality of process outputs by identifying and removing the causes of defects (errors) and variation in manufacturing and business processes. It uses a set of quality management methods, including statistical methods, and creates a special infrastructure of people within the organization ('Black Belts' etc.)

   a. 8.3 filename
   b. 68-95-99.7 rule
   c. Back-end database
   d. Six Sigma

4. _____ in project management is a tangible or intangible object produced as a result of project execution, as part of an obligation. The term can be either a noun: an item, product or artifact which must be created and then delivered as part of an obligation, or an adjective: describing something which must be delivered as part of an obligation. Like many terms common in corporate usage, the word is considered corporate jargon or corporatese, referring specifically to goals.

a. Deliverable
b. Negative volume index
c. Pivot point calculations
d. 68-95-99.7 rule

5. A _____ is a professional in the field of project management. _____s can have the responsibility of the planning, execution, and closing of any project, typically relating to construction industry, architecture, computer networking, telecommunications or software development.

Many other fields in the production, design and service industries also have _____s.

a. Project manager
b. Logical framework approach
c. Project management office
d. Schedule chicken

6. In project management, a _____ is a subset of a project that can be assigned to a specific party for execution. Because of the similarity, _____s are often misidentified as projects.

Similar to a work breakdown structure, a _____ is part of a Plan Breakdown Structure, representing a collection of work actions necessary to create a specific result.

a. Risk register
b. Precedence Diagram Method
c. Work package
d. Constructability

7. _____ is a term used in subtly different ways in a number of fields, including philosophy, physics, statistics, economics, finance, insurance, psychology, sociology, engineering, and information science. It applies to predictions of future events, to physical measurements already made, or to the unknown.

In his seminal work Risk, _____, and Profit University of Chicago economist Frank Knight (1921) established the important distinction between risk and _____:

'_____ must be taken in a sense radically distinct from the familiar notion of risk, from which it has never been properly separated....

a. ACID
b. Uncertainty
c. AACE International
d. AACR2

Chapter 2. Strategic Management and Project Selection

1. The _____ in a business or professional enterprise is the department or group that defines and maintains the standards of process, generally related to project management, within the organization. The _____ strives to standardize and introduce economies of repetition in the execution of projects. The _____ is the source of documentation, guidance and metrics on the practice of project management and execution.

    a. Commissioning Management Systems
    b. Project management office
    c. Project triangle
    d. Nonlinear Management

2. A command center (often called a _____) is any place that is used to provide centralised command for some purpose. While frequently considered to be a military facility, these can be used in many other cases by governments or businesses. The term '_____' is also often used in politics to refer to teams of communications people who monitor and listen to the media and the public, respond to inquiries, and synthesize opinions to determine the best course of action.

    a. Report2Web
    b. Social Return on Investment
    c. Salesforce.com
    d. War room

3. The _____ in software engineering is a model of the maturity of the capability of certain business processes. A maturity model can be described as a structured collection of elements that describe certain aspects of maturity in an organization, and aids in the definition and understanding of an organization's processes. The _____ has been superseded by the _____ Integration (Capability Maturity Modell.)

    a. Back-end database
    b. 8.3 filename
    c. 68-95-99.7 rule
    d. Capability Maturity Model

4. _____ is the discipline of planning, organizing and managing resources to bring about the successful completion of specific project goals and objectives.

    A project is a finite endeavor--having specific start and completion dates--undertaken to meet particular goals and objectives, usually to bring about beneficial change or added value. This finite characteristic of projects stands in contrast to processes, or operations--which is repetitive, permanent or semi-permanent functional work to produce products or services.

    a. SMART
    b. Risk register
    c. Logical framework approach
    d. Project Management

Chapter 2. Strategic Management and Project Selection

5. _____ is part of project management, which relates to the use of schedules such as Gantt charts to plan and subsequently report progress within the project environment.

Initially, the project scope is defined and the appropriate methods for completing the project are determined. Following this step, the durations for the various tasks necessary to complete the work are listed and grouped into a work breakdown structure.

   a. Cone of Uncertainty
   b. Project plan
   c. Project manager
   d. Project planning

6. _____ in organizations and public policy is both the organizational process of creating and maintaining a plan; and the psychological process of thinking about the activities required to create a desired goal on some scale. As such, it is a fundamental property of intelligent behavior. This thought process is essential to the creation and refinement of a plan, or integration of it with other plans, that is, it combines forecasting of developments with the preparation of scenarios of how to react to them.

   a. 68-95-99.7 rule
   b. Back-end database
   c. 8.3 filename
   d. Planning

7. _____ in project management refers to uncontrolled changes in a project's scope. This phenomenon can occur when the scope of a project is not properly defined, documented, or controlled. It is generally considered a negative occurrence that is to be avoided.

   a. Problem domain analysis
   b. Graphical Evaluation and Review Technique
   c. Student syndrome
   d. Scope creep

8. _____ is a general algorithm for finding optimal solutions of various optimization problems, especially in discrete and combinatorial optimization. It consists of a systematic enumeration of all candidate solutions, where large subsets of fruitless candidates are discarded en masse, by using upper and lower estimated bounds of the quantity being optimized.

The method was first proposed by A. H. Land and A. G. Doig in 1960 for linear programming.

Chapter 2. Strategic Management and Project Selection

a. 8.3 filename
b. Branch and bound
c. Back-end database
d. 68-95-99.7 rule

9. _____ constitute a class of computer-based information systems including knowledge-based systems that support decision-making activities.

_____ are a specific class of computerized information systems that supports business and organizational decision-making activities. A properly-designed _____ is an interactive software-based system intended to help decision makers compile useful information from raw data, documents, personal knowledge, and/or business models to identify and solve problems and make decisions.

a. 8.3 filename
b. Back-end database
c. 68-95-99.7 rule
d. Decision support systems

10. _____ is a term used in subtly different ways in a number of fields, including philosophy, physics, statistics, economics, finance, insurance, psychology, sociology, engineering, and information science. It applies to predictions of future events, to physical measurements already made, or to the unknown.

In his seminal work Risk, _____, and Profit University of Chicago economist Frank Knight (1921) established the important distinction between risk and _____:

'_____ must be taken in a sense radically distinct from the familiar notion of risk, from which it has never been properly separated....

a. AACR2
b. ACID
c. AACE International
d. Uncertainty

11. _____ is a technical analysis term used to compare performances of different trading systems or different investments within one system. Note, it is not simply another word for profit. There are varying definitions for it, some as simple as the expected or average ratio of revenue to cost for a particular investment or trading system or 'ratio of the number of winning trades or investments to the total number of trades or investments made, a number ranging from zero to 1.' Others can be complex or counter-intuitive.

a. 68-95-99.7 rule
b. Back-end database
c. Saleability
d. 8.3 filename

12. The _____ is a systematic, interactive forecasting method which relies on a panel of independent experts. The carefully selected experts answer questionnaires in two or more rounds. After each round, a facilitator provides an anonymous summary of the experts' forecasts from the previous round as well as the reasons they provided for their judgments.

   a. Learning organization
   b. Group decision support systems
   c. Service innovation
   d. Delphi method

13. The _____ is a structured technique for dealing with complex decisions. Rather than prescribing a 'correct' decision, the _____ helps the decision makers find the one that best suits their needs and their understanding of the problem.

Based on mathematics and psychology, it was developed by Thomas L. Saaty in the 1970s and has been extensively studied and refined since then.

   a. AACE International
   b. ACID
   c. AACR2
   d. Analytic hierarchy process

14. In probability theory and statistics, the _____ (or expectation value or mean and for continuous random variables with a density function it is the probability density -weighted integral of the possible values.

The term '_____' can be misleading.

   a. ACID
   b. AACR2
   c. AACE International
   d. Expected value

15. _____ is the identification, assessment, and prioritization of risks followed by coordinated and economical application of resources to minimize, monitor, and control the probability and/or impact of unfortunate events.. Risks can come from uncertainty in financial markets, project failures, legal liabilities, credit risk, accidents, natural causes and disasters as well as deliberate attacks from an adversary. Several _____ standards have been developed including the Project Management Institute, the National Institute of Science and Technology, actuarial societies, and ISO standards.
   a. Regression toward the mean
   b. Stitch Pipeline
   c. Signals intelligence
   d. Risk Management

16. _____ is the study of how the variation (uncertainty) in the output of a mathematical model can be apportioned, qualitatively or quantitatively, to different sources of variation in the input of a model .

In more general terms uncertainty and sensitivity analyses investigate the robustness of a study when the study includes some form of mathematical modelling. While uncertainty analysis studies the overall uncertainty in the conclusions of the study, _____ tries to identify what source of uncertainty weights more on the study's conclusions.

   a. Product life cycle
   b. Sensitivity analysis
   c. Product support
   d. Business Technology Management

17. An _____ is the process of creating development goals and objectives and using these goals and objectives to improve productivity as well as development capabilities. The purpose of this process is generally to ensure that each project will accomplish its development goals and objectives. Projects can be differentiated into five types of projects: breakthrough, platform, derivative, R'D, or partnered projects (such as projects performed with partners or allianced firms.)
   a. AACR2
   b. ACID
   c. AACE International
   d. Aggregate project plan

18. A _____, according to the Project Management Body of Knowledge, is

   '...a formal, approved document used to guide both project execution and project control. The primary uses of the _____ are to document planning assumptions and decisions, facilitate communication among stakeholders, and document approved scope, cost, and schedule baselines. A _____ may be summarized or detailed.'

Chapter 2. Strategic Management and Project Selection

PRINCE2 defines

'...a statement of how and when a project's objectives are to be achieved, by showing the major products, milestones, activities and resources required on the project.'

In some industries, particularly information technology, the term '_____' can refer to a Gantt chart or other document that shows project activities along a timeline.

a. Critical Chain
b. Project plan
c. Hammock activity
d. Responsibility assignment matrix

19. A _____ is a standard business process whose purpose is to invite suppliers into a bidding process to bid on specific products or services.

An _____ typically involves more than the price per item. Information like payment terms, quality level per item or contract length are possible to be requested during the bidding process.

a. Back-end database
b. 68-95-99.7 rule
c. 8.3 filename
d. Request for Quotation

20. _____ is used to assign the available resources in an economic way. It is part of resource management.

In strategic planning, is a plan for using available resources, for example human resources, especially in the near term, to achieve goals for the future.

a. 8.3 filename
b. Back-end database
c. 68-95-99.7 rule
d. Resource allocation

Chapter 3. The Project Manager

1. A _____ is a professional in the field of project management. _____s can have the responsibility of the planning, execution, and closing of any project, typically relating to construction industry, architecture, computer networking, telecommunications or software development.

Many other fields in the production, design and service industries also have _____s.

   a. Schedule chicken
   b. Project management office
   c. Logical framework approach
   d. Project manager

2. _____ is the discipline of planning, organizing and managing resources to bring about the successful completion of specific project goals and objectives.

A project is a finite endeavor--having specific start and completion dates--undertaken to meet particular goals and objectives, usually to bring about beneficial change or added value. This finite characteristic of projects stands in contrast to processes, or operations--which is repetitive, permanent or semi-permanent functional work to produce products or services.

   a. Project management
   b. Logical framework approach
   c. Risk register
   d. SMART

3. In business management, _____ is a management style where a manager closely observes or controls the work of his or her subordinates or employees. _____ is generally used as a negative term.

Webster's Dictionary defines micromanage as: 'to manage with great or excessive control, or attention to details'.

   a. Managing stage boundaries
   b. Workflow Management Coalition
   c. Micromanagement
   d. Mentorship

4. In a general sense, the term _____ refers to a system of people, data records and activities that process the data and information in an organization, and it includes the organization's manual and automated processes. In a narrow sense, the term _____ refers to the specific application software that is used to store data records in a computer system and automates some of the information-processing activities of the organization. Computer-based _____s are in the field of information technology.

Chapter 3. The Project Manager

a. AACE International
b. Information system
c. ACID
d. AACR2

5. A _____ is a subset of the overall internal controls of a business covering the application of people, documents, technologies, and procedures by management accountants to solving business problems such as costing a product, service or a business-wide strategy. _____s are distinct from regular information systems in that they are used to analyze other information systems applied in operational activities in the organization. Academically, the term is commonly used to refer to the group of information management methods tied to the automation or support of human decision making, e.g. Decision Support Systems, Expert systems, and Executive information systems.

   a. Hierarchical storage management
   b. RODIN Data Asset Management
   c. Strategic information system
   d. Management information system

6. In probability theory and statistics, the _____ is a continuous probability distribution with lower limit a, mode c and upper limit b.

$$f(x|a,b,c) = \begin{cases} \frac{2(x-a)}{(b-a)(c-a)} & \text{for } a \leq x \leq c \\ \frac{2(b-x)}{(b-a)(b-c)} & \text{for } c \leq x \leq b \\ 0 & \text{otherwise} \end{cases}$$

The distribution simplifies when c = a or c = b. For example, if a = 0, b = 1 and c = 1, then the equations above become:

$$\left. \begin{array}{rcl} f(x) & = & 2x \\ F(x) & = & x^2 \end{array} \right\} \text{ for } 0 \leq x \leq 1$$

$$E(X) = \frac{2}{3}$$

$$\text{Var}(X) = \frac{1}{18}$$

This distribution for a = 0, b = 1 and c = 0.5 is distribution of $X = (X_1 + X_2)/2$, where X_1, X_2 are two independent random variables with standard uniform distribution.

a. Triangular distribution
b. Back-end database
c. 68-95-99.7 rule
d. 8.3 filename

7. _____ is a term used in subtly different ways in a number of fields, including philosophy, physics, statistics, economics, finance, insurance, psychology, sociology, engineering, and information science. It applies to predictions of future events, to physical measurements already made, or to the unknown.

In his seminal work Risk, _____, and Profit University of Chicago economist Frank Knight (1921) established the important distinction between risk and _____:

'_____ must be taken in a sense radically distinct from the familiar notion of risk, from which it has never been properly separated....

a. ACID
b. AACR2
c. AACE International
d. Uncertainty

8. _____ in project management refers to uncontrolled changes in a project's scope. This phenomenon can occur when the scope of a project is not properly defined, documented, or controlled. It is generally considered a negative occurrence that is to be avoided.
a. Problem domain analysis
b. Scope creep
c. Graphical Evaluation and Review Technique
d. Student syndrome

9. _____ in organizations and public policy is both the organizational process of creating and maintaining a plan; and the psychological process of thinking about the activities required to create a desired goal on some scale. As such, it is a fundamental property of intelligent behavior. This thought process is essential to the creation and refinement of a plan, or integration of it with other plans, that is, it combines forecasting of developments with the preparation of scenarios of how to react to them.

a. 68-95-99.7 rule
b. Planning
c. Back-end database
d. 8.3 filename

10. _____ occurs when the output of a system acts to oppose changes to the input of the system; with the result that the changes are attenuated. If the overall feedback of the system is negative, then the system will tend to be stable.

In many physical and biological systems, qualitatively different influences can oppose each other.

a. 8.3 filename
b. Back-end database
c. 68-95-99.7 rule
d. Negative feedback

11. The general definition of an _____ is an evaluation of a person, organization, system, process, project or product. _____s are performed to ascertain the validity and reliability of information; also to provide an assessment of a system's internal control. The goal of an _____ is to express an opinion on the person / organization/system (etc) in question, under evaluation based on work done on a test basis.
a. ACID
b. Audit
c. AACE International
d. AACR2

12. Moral psychology is a field of study in both philosophy and psychology. Some use the term 'moral psychology' relatively narrowly to refer to the study of moral development. However, others tend to use the term more broadly to include any topics at the intersection of _____ and psychology (and philosophy of mind.)
a. AACR2
b. AACE International
c. ACID
d. Ethics

13. A _____ is a team whose members usually belong to different groups, functions and are assigned to activities for the same project. A team can be divided into sub-teams according to need. Usually _____s are only used for a defined period of time.

a. Project team
b. Project manager
c. Certified project manager
d. Project management 2.0

Chapter 4. Project Organization

1. _____ is a type of organizational management in which people with similar skills are pooled for work assignments. For example, all engineers may be in one engineering department and report to an engineering manager, but these same engineers may be assigned to different projects and report to a project manager while working on that project. Therefore, each engineer may have to work under several managers to get their job done.

   a. Workflow Management Coalition
   b. Micromanagement
   c. Managing stage boundaries
   d. Matrix Management

2. _____ is the discipline of planning, organizing and managing resources to bring about the successful completion of specific project goals and objectives.

   A project is a finite endeavor--having specific start and completion dates--undertaken to meet particular goals and objectives, usually to bring about beneficial change or added value. This finite characteristic of projects stands in contrast to processes, or operations--which is repetitive, permanent or semi-permanent functional work to produce products or services.

   a. Logical framework approach
   b. Risk register
   c. SMART
   d. Project management

3. _____ occurs when the output of a system acts to oppose changes to the input of the system; with the result that the changes are attenuated. If the overall feedback of the system is negative, then the system will tend to be stable.

   In many physical and biological systems, qualitatively different influences can oppose each other.

   a. Back-end database
   b. 8.3 filename
   c. 68-95-99.7 rule
   d. Negative feedback

4. _____ is the identification, assessment, and prioritization of risks followed by coordinated and economical application of resources to minimize, monitor, and control the probability and/or impact of unfortunate events.. Risks can come from uncertainty in financial markets, project failures, legal liabilities, credit risk, accidents, natural causes and disasters as well as deliberate attacks from an adversary. Several _____ standards have been developed including the Project Management Institute, the National Institute of Science and Technology, actuarial societies, and ISO standards.

Chapter 4. Project Organization

a. Signals intelligence
b. Stitch Pipeline
c. Regression toward the mean
d. Risk Management

5. The _____ in a business or professional enterprise is the department or group that defines and maintains the standards of process, generally related to project management, within the organization. The _____ strives to standardize and introduce economies of repetition in the execution of projects. The _____ is the source of documentation, guidance and metrics on the practice of project management and execution.

a. Project management office
b. Commissioning Management Systems
c. Nonlinear Management
d. Project triangle

6. A _____ is a professional in the field of project management. _____s can have the responsibility of the planning, execution, and closing of any project, typically relating to construction industry, architecture, computer networking, telecommunications or software development.

Many other fields in the production, design and service industries also have _____s.

a. Logical framework approach
b. Project management office
c. Schedule chicken
d. Project manager

7. A command center (often called a _____) is any place that is used to provide centralised command for some purpose. While frequently considered to be a military facility, these can be used in many other cases by governments or businesses. The term '_____' is also often used in politics to refer to teams of communications people who monitor and listen to the media and the public, respond to inquiries, and synthesize opinions to determine the best course of action.

a. Salesforce.com
b. Social Return on Investment
c. War room
d. Report2Web

8. _____ is a term used in subtly different ways in a number of fields, including philosophy, physics, statistics, economics, finance, insurance, psychology, sociology, engineering, and information science. It applies to predictions of future events, to physical measurements already made, or to the unknown.

Chapter 4. Project Organization

In his seminal work Risk, _____, and Profit University of Chicago economist Frank Knight (1921) established the important distinction between risk and _____:

'_____ must be taken in a sense radically distinct from the familiar notion of risk, from which it has never been properly separated....

  a. AACR2
  b. AACE International
  c. ACID
  d. Uncertainty

9. A _____ in project management and systems engineering, is a tool used to define and group a project's discrete work elements (or tasks) in a way that helps organize and define the total work scope of the project.

A _____ element may be a product, data, a service, or any combination. A _____ also provides the necessary framework for detailed cost estimating and control along with providing guidance for schedule development and control.

  a. Back-end database
  b. 68-95-99.7 rule
  c. Work breakdown structure
  d. 8.3 filename

10. _____ is a business management strategy, initially implemented by Motorola, that today enjoys widespread application in many sectors of industry.

_____ seeks to improve the quality of process outputs by identifying and removing the causes of defects (errors) and variation in manufacturing and business processes. It uses a set of quality management methods, including statistical methods, and creates a special infrastructure of people within the organization ('Black Belts' etc.)

  a. 8.3 filename
  b. Back-end database
  c. 68-95-99.7 rule
  d. Six Sigma

Chapter 5. Project Planning

1. _____ in organizations and public policy is both the organizational process of creating and maintaining a plan; and the psychological process of thinking about the activities required to create a desired goal on some scale. As such, it is a fundamental property of intelligent behavior. This thought process is essential to the creation and refinement of a plan, or integration of it with other plans, that is, it combines forecasting of developments with the preparation of scenarios of how to react to them.
   a. 8.3 filename
   b. Back-end database
   c. 68-95-99.7 rule
   d. Planning

2. _____ is the discipline of planning, organizing and managing resources to bring about the successful completion of specific project goals and objectives.

   A project is a finite endeavor--having specific start and completion dates--undertaken to meet particular goals and objectives, usually to bring about beneficial change or added value. This finite characteristic of projects stands in contrast to processes, or operations--which is repetitive, permanent or semi-permanent functional work to produce products or services.

   a. Risk register
   b. Project Management
   c. Logical framework approach
   d. SMART

3. _____ in project management is a tangible or intangible object produced as a result of project execution, as part of an obligation. The term can be either a noun: an item, product or artifact which must be created and then delivered as part of an obligation, or an adjective: describing something which must be delivered as part of an obligation. Like many terms common in corporate usage, the word is considered corporate jargon or corporatese, referring specifically to goals.
   a. Pivot point calculations
   b. Deliverable
   c. Negative volume index
   d. 68-95-99.7 rule

4. A _____, according to the Project Management Body of Knowledge, is

   '...a formal, approved document used to guide both project execution and project control. The primary uses of the _____ are to document planning assumptions and decisions, facilitate communication among stakeholders, and document approved scope, cost, and schedule baselines. A _____ may be summarized or detailed.'

Chapter 5. Project Planning

PRINCE2 defines

'...a statement of how and when a project's objectives are to be achieved, by showing the major products, milestones, activities and resources required on the project.'

In some industries, particularly information technology, the term '_____' can refer to a Gantt chart or other document that shows project activities along a timeline.

a. Hammock activity
b. Project plan
c. Critical Chain
d. Responsibility assignment matrix

5. A _____ in project management and systems engineering, is a tool used to define and group a project's discrete work elements (or tasks) in a way that helps organize and define the total work scope of the project.

A _____ element may be a product, data, a service, or any combination. A _____ also provides the necessary framework for detailed cost estimating and control along with providing guidance for schedule development and control.

a. Work breakdown structure
b. Back-end database
c. 68-95-99.7 rule
d. 8.3 filename

6. _____ is the identification, assessment, and prioritization of risks followed by coordinated and economical application of resources to minimize, monitor, and control the probability and/or impact of unfortunate events.. Risks can come from uncertainty in financial markets, project failures, legal liabilities, credit risk, accidents, natural causes and disasters as well as deliberate attacks from an adversary. Several _____ standards have been developed including the Project Management Institute, the National Institute of Science and Technology, actuarial societies, and ISO standards.

a. Signals intelligence
b. Risk management
c. Regression toward the mean
d. Stitch Pipeline

7. A _____ is a document prepared by a project manager to foresee risks, to estimate the effectiveness, and to create response plans to mitigate them. It also consists of the risk assessment matrix.

Chapter 5. Project Planning

A risk is defined as 'an uncertain event or condition that, if it occurs, has a positive or negative effect on a project's objectives.' Risk is inherent with any project, and project managers should assess risks continually and develop plans to address them.

a. Time horizon
b. Product description
c. Risk management plan
d. Product breakdown structure

8. _____ is a work methodology based on the parallelization of tasks (ie. concurrently.) It refers to an approach used in product development in which functions of design engineering, manufacturing engineering and other functions are integrated to reduce the elapsed time required to bring a new product to the market.
   a. Project Management Simulator
   b. Cone of Uncertainty
   c. Product description
   d. Concurrent engineering

9. The general definition of an _____ is an evaluation of a person, organization, system, process, project or product. _____s are performed to ascertain the validity and reliability of information; also to provide an assessment of a system's internal control. The goal of an _____ is to express an opinion on the person / organization/system (etc) in question, under evaluation based on work done on a test basis.
   a. ACID
   b. Audit
   c. AACE International
   d. AACR2

10. A _____ is a type of bar chart that illustrates a project schedule. _____s illustrate the start and finish dates of the terminal elements and summary elements of a project. Terminal elements and summary elements comprise the work breakdown structure of the project.
    a. 8.3 filename
    b. Back-end database
    c. Gantt chart
    d. 68-95-99.7 rule

11. _____ is a systematic method to improve the 'value' of goods or products and services by using an examination of function. Value, as defined, is the ratio of function to cost. Value can therefore be increased by either improving the function or reducing the cost.

Chapter 5. Project Planning

a. 68-95-99.7 rule
b. Back-end database
c. 8.3 filename
d. Value engineering

12. _____ is a list of the raw materials, sub-assemblies, intermediate assemblies, sub-components, components, parts and the quantities of each needed to manufacture an end item (final product).

a. 8.3 filename
b. Bill of materials
c. Back-end database
d. 68-95-99.7 rule

13. In project management, a _____ is a subset of a project that can be assigned to a specific party for execution. Because of the similarity, _____s are often misidentified as projects.

Similar to a work breakdown structure, a _____ is part of a Plan Breakdown Structure, representing a collection of work actions necessary to create a specific result.

a. Precedence Diagram Method
b. Constructability
c. Risk register
d. Work package

14. In business management, _____ is a management style where a manager closely observes or controls the work of his or her subordinates or employees. _____ is generally used as a negative term.

Webster's Dictionary defines micromanage as: 'to manage with great or excessive control, or attention to details'.

a. Mentorship
b. Workflow Management Coalition
c. Managing stage boundaries
d. Micromanagement

15. _____ occurs when the output of a system acts to oppose changes to the input of the system; with the result that the changes are attenuated. If the overall feedback of the system is negative, then the system will tend to be stable.

In many physical and biological systems, qualitatively different influences can oppose each other.

a. 8.3 filename
b. 68-95-99.7 rule
c. Back-end database
d. Negative feedback

16. In a general sense, the term _____ refers to a system of people, data records and activities that process the data and information in an organization, and it includes the organization's manual and automated processes. In a narrow sense, the term _____ refers to the specific application software that is used to store data records in a computer system and automates some of the information-processing activities of the organization. Computer-based _____s are in the field of information technology.

   a. Information system
   b. AACE International
   c. ACID
   d. AACR2

17. The term '_____' refers to the concept of collecting information and attempting to spot a pattern in the information. In some fields of study, the term '_____' has more formally-defined meanings.

In project management _____ is a mathematical technique that uses historical results to predict future outcome.

   a. Partial least squares regression
   b. Multivariate adaptive regression splines
   c. Probit model
   d. Trend analysis

Chapter 6. Conflict and Negotiation

1. Moral psychology is a field of study in both philosophy and psychology. Some use the term 'moral psychology' relatively narrowly to refer to the study of moral development. However, others tend to use the term more broadly to include any topics at the intersection of _____ and psychology (and philosophy of mind.)
    a. AACE International
    b. AACR2
    c. ACID
    d. Ethics

2. _____ occurs when the output of a system acts to oppose changes to the input of the system; with the result that the changes are attenuated. If the overall feedback of the system is negative, then the system will tend to be stable.

In many physical and biological systems, qualitatively different influences can oppose each other.

   a. Back-end database
   b. 8.3 filename
   c. Negative feedback
   d. 68-95-99.7 rule

3. _____ in organizations and public policy is both the organizational process of creating and maintaining a plan; and the psychological process of thinking about the activities required to create a desired goal on some scale. As such, it is a fundamental property of intelligent behavior. This thought process is essential to the creation and refinement of a plan, or integration of it with other plans, that is, it combines forecasting of developments with the preparation of scenarios of how to react to them.
    a. 8.3 filename
    b. Planning
    c. Back-end database
    d. 68-95-99.7 rule

4. _____ is a term used in subtly different ways in a number of fields, including philosophy, physics, statistics, economics, finance, insurance, psychology, sociology, engineering, and information science. It applies to predictions of future events, to physical measurements already made, or to the unknown.

In his seminal work Risk, _____, and Profit University of Chicago economist Frank Knight (1921) established the important distinction between risk and _____:

> '_____ must be taken in a sense radically distinct from the familiar notion of risk, from which it has never been properly separated....

a. Uncertainty
b. ACID
c. AACE International
d. AACR2

5. _____ is a type of organizational management in which people with similar skills are pooled for work assignments. For example, all engineers may be in one engineering department and report to an engineering manager, but these same engineers may be assigned to different projects and report to a project manager while working on that project. Therefore, each engineer may have to work under several managers to get their job done.

 a. Managing stage boundaries
 b. Matrix Management
 c. Micromanagement
 d. Workflow Management Coalition

6. A _____ is a professional in the field of project management. _____s can have the responsibility of the planning, execution, and closing of any project, typically relating to construction industry, architecture, computer networking, telecommunications or software development.

Many other fields in the production, design and service industries also have _____s.

 a. Project management office
 b. Logical framework approach
 c. Schedule chicken
 d. Project manager

7. _____ is the discipline of planning, organizing and managing resources to bring about the successful completion of specific project goals and objectives.

A project is a finite endeavor--having specific start and completion dates--undertaken to meet particular goals and objectives, usually to bring about beneficial change or added value. This finite characteristic of projects stands in contrast to processes, or operations--which is repetitive, permanent or semi-permanent functional work to produce products or services.

 a. SMART
 b. Logical framework approach
 c. Risk register
 d. Project management

Chapter 7. Budgeting and Cost Estimation 25

1. _____ is the calculated approximation of a result which is usable even if input data may be incomplete or uncertain.

In statistics, see _____ theory, estimator.

In mathematics, approximation or _____ typically means finding upper or lower bounds of a quantity that cannot readily be computed precisely and is also an educated guess.

   a. ACID
   b. AACE International
   c. AACR2
   d. Estimation

2. In databases and transaction processing, _____, (2PL) is a concurrency control locking protocol which guarantees serializability. It is also the name of the resulting class (set) of transaction schedules. Using locks that block processes, 2PL may be subject to deadlocks that result from the mutual blocking of two transactions or more.
   a. 68-95-99.7 rule
   b. Back-end database
   c. Two-phase locking
   d. 8.3 filename

3. _____ is a term used in subtly different ways in a number of fields, including philosophy, physics, statistics, economics, finance, insurance, psychology, sociology, engineering, and information science. It applies to predictions of future events, to physical measurements already made, or to the unknown.

In his seminal work Risk, _____, and Profit University of Chicago economist Frank Knight (1921) established the important distinction between risk and _____:

   '_____ must be taken in a sense radically distinct from the familiar notion of risk, from which it has never been properly separated....

   a. AACR2
   b. Uncertainty
   c. AACE International
   d. ACID

4. A _____ in project management and systems engineering, is a tool used to define and group a project's discrete work elements (or tasks) in a way that helps organize and define the total work scope of the project.

Chapter 7. Budgeting and Cost Estimation

A _____ element may be a product, data, a service, or any combination. A _____ also provides the necessary framework for detailed cost estimating and control along with providing guidance for schedule development and control.

a. 68-95-99.7 rule
b. Work breakdown structure
c. Back-end database
d. 8.3 filename

5. _____ is the process of estimation in unknown situations. Prediction is a similar, but more general term. Both can refer to estimation of time series, cross-sectional or longitudinal data.
a. Power transform
b. Photoanalysis
c. Local convex hull
d. Forecasting

6. A _____ is a principle with broad application that is not intended to be strictly accurate or reliable for every situation. It is an easily learned and easily applied procedure for approximately calculating or recalling some value, or for making some determination. Compare this to heuristic, a similar concept used in mathematical discourse, psychology and computer science, particularly in algorithm design.
a. Back-end database
b. Rule of thumb
c. 8.3 filename
d. 68-95-99.7 rule

7. _____ in organizations and public policy is both the organizational process of creating and maintaining a plan; and the psychological process of thinking about the activities required to create a desired goal on some scale. As such, it is a fundamental property of intelligent behavior. This thought process is essential to the creation and refinement of a plan, or integration of it with other plans, that is, it combines forecasting of developments with the preparation of scenarios of how to react to them.
a. 68-95-99.7 rule
b. Back-end database
c. 8.3 filename
d. Planning

8. _____ occurs when the output of a system acts to oppose changes to the input of the system; with the result that the changes are attenuated. If the overall feedback of the system is negative, then the system will tend to be stable.

Chapter 7. Budgeting and Cost Estimation

In many physical and biological systems, qualitatively different influences can oppose each other.

a. 68-95-99.7 rule
b. Back-end database
c. Negative feedback
d. 8.3 filename

9. _____ is a systematic method to improve the 'value' of goods or products and services by using an examination of function. Value, as defined, is the ratio of function to cost. Value can therefore be increased by either improving the function or reducing the cost.
    a. 8.3 filename
    b. Value engineering
    c. 68-95-99.7 rule
    d. Back-end database

10. Moral psychology is a field of study in both philosophy and psychology. Some use the term 'moral psychology' relatively narrowly to refer to the study of moral development. However, others tend to use the term more broadly to include any topics at the intersection of _____ and psychology (and philosophy of mind.)
    a. AACR2
    b. ACID
    c. AACE International
    d. Ethics

11. _____ is the discipline of planning, organizing and managing resources to bring about the successful completion of specific project goals and objectives.

A project is a finite endeavor--having specific start and completion dates--undertaken to meet particular goals and objectives, usually to bring about beneficial change or added value. This finite characteristic of projects stands in contrast to processes, or operations--which is repetitive, permanent or semi-permanent functional work to produce products or services.

   a. Logical framework approach
   b. SMART
   c. Risk register
   d. Project Management

Chapter 7. Budgeting and Cost Estimation

12. _____ is the budgeting system that, contrary to conventional budgeting, describes and gives the detailed costs of every activity or programme that is to be carried out in a budget.

Objectives, outputs and expected results are described fully as are their necessary resource costs, for example, raw materials, equipment and staff. The sum of all activities or programmes constitute the Programme Budget.

   a. 68-95-99.7 rule
   b. 8.3 filename
   c. Back-end database
   d. Programme budgeting

13. _____s are expenses that change in proportion to the activity of a business. In other words, _____ is the sum of marginal costs. It can also be considered normal costs.
   a. 68-95-99.7 rule
   b. Back-end database
   c. 8.3 filename
   d. Variable cost

14. Models of the _____ effect and the closely related experience curve effect express the relationship between equations for experience and efficiency or between efficiency gains and investment in the effort. The experience of '_____s' was first observed by the 19th Century German psychologist Hermann Ebbinghaus according to the difficulty of memorizing varying numbers of verbal stimuli, and subsequent learning about the complex processes of learning are discussed in the

The rule used for representing the _____ effect states that the more times a task has been performed, the less time will be required on each subsequent iteration.

   a. 68-95-99.7 rule
   b. Back-end database
   c. 8.3 filename
   d. Learning curve

15. _____ in project management refers to uncontrolled changes in a project's scope. This phenomenon can occur when the scope of a project is not properly defined, documented, or controlled. It is generally considered a negative occurrence that is to be avoided.

Chapter 7. Budgeting and Cost Estimation

a. Graphical Evaluation and Review Technique
b. Student syndrome
c. Problem domain analysis
d. Scope creep

16. In probability theory and statistics, the _____ (or expectation value or mean and for continuous random variables with a density function it is the probability density -weighted integral of the possible values.

The term '_____' can be misleading.

a. ACID
b. AACR2
c. AACE International
d. Expected value

17. The _____ or simply average deviation of a data set is the average of the absolute deviations and is a summary statistic of statistical dispersion or variability. It is also called the mean absolute deviation, but this is easily confused with the median absolute deviation.

The average absolute deviation of a set $\{x_1, x_2, ..., x_n\}$ is

$$\frac{1}{n}\sum_{i=1}^{n} |x_i - m(X)|$$

The choice of measure of central tendency, m(X), has a marked effect on the value of the average deviation.

a. AACR2
b. Average absolute deviation,
c. AACE International
d. ACID

18. _____ is a business management strategy aimed at embedding awareness of quality in all organizational processes. _____ has been widely used in manufacturing, education, hospitals, call centers, government, and service industries, as well as NASA space and science programs.

Chapter 7. Budgeting and Cost Estimation

When used together as a phrase, the three words in this expression have the following meanings:

- Total: Involving the entire organization, supply chain, and/or product life cycle
- Quality: With its usual definitions, with all its complexities
- Management: The system of managing with steps like Plan, Organize, Control, Lead, Staff, provisioning and organizing.

As defined by the International Organization for Standardization (ISO):

'_____ is a management approach for an organization, centered on quality, based on the participation of all its members and aiming at long-term success through customer satisfaction, and benefits to all members of the organization and to society.' ISO 8402:1994

One major aim is to reduce variation from every process so that greater consistency of effort is obtained. (Royse, D., Thyer, B., Padgett D., ' Logan T., 2006)

In Japan, _____ comprises four process steps, namely:

1. Kaizen - Focuses on 'Continuous Process Improvement', to make processes visible, repeatable and measurable.
2. Atarimae Hinshitsu - The idea that 'things will work as they are supposed to' .
3. Kansei - Examining the way the user applies the product leads to improvement in the product itself.
4. Miryokuteki Hinshitsu - The idea that 'things should have an aesthetic quality' (for example, a pen will write in a way that is pleasing to the writer.)

_____ requires that the company maintain this quality standard in all aspects of its business. This requires ensuring that things are done right the first time and that defects and waste are eliminated from operations.

a. 8.3 filename
b. Back-end database
c. 68-95-99.7 rule
d. TQM

Chapter 8. Scheduling

1. A _____ is a type of bar chart that illustrates a project schedule. _____s illustrate the start and finish dates of the terminal elements and summary elements of a project. Terminal elements and summary elements comprise the work breakdown structure of the project.
    a. Back-end database
    b. Gantt chart
    c. 68-95-99.7 rule
    d. 8.3 filename

2. _____ is used to assign the available resources in an economic way. It is part of resource management.

In strategic planning,is a plan for using available resources, for example human resources, especially in the near term, to achieve goals for the future.

   a. Back-end database
   b. 8.3 filename
   c. 68-95-99.7 rule
   d. Resource allocation

3. In databases and transaction processing, _____, (2PL) is a concurrency control locking protocol which guarantees serializability. It is also the name of the resulting class (set) of transaction schedules. Using locks that block processes, 2PL may be subject to deadlocks that result from the mutual blocking of two transactions or more.
   a. 68-95-99.7 rule
   b. Back-end database
   c. 8.3 filename
   d. Two-phase locking

4. _____ in organizations and public policy is both the organizational process of creating and maintaining a plan; and the psychological process of thinking about the activities required to create a desired goal on some scale. As such, it is a fundamental property of intelligent behavior. This thought process is essential to the creation and refinement of a plan, or integration of it with other plans, that is, it combines forecasting of developments with the preparation of scenarios of how to react to them.
   a. Back-end database
   b. Planning
   c. 68-95-99.7 rule
   d. 8.3 filename

5. A _____, according to the Project Management Body of Knowledge, is

Chapter 8. Scheduling

'...a formal, approved document used to guide both project execution and project control. The primary uses of the _____ are to document planning assumptions and decisions, facilitate communication among stakeholders, and document approved scope, cost, and schedule baselines. A _____ may be summarized or detailed.'

PRINCE2 defines

'...a statement of how and when a project's objectives are to be achieved, by showing the major products, milestones, activities and resources required on the project.'

In some industries, particularly information technology, the term '_____' can refer to a Gantt chart or other document that shows project activities along a timeline.

a. Critical Chain
b. Hammock activity
c. Project plan
d. Responsibility assignment matrix

6. A _____ in project management and systems engineering, is a tool used to define and group a project's discrete work elements (or tasks) in a way that helps organize and define the total work scope of the project.

A _____ element may be a product, data, a service, or any combination. A _____ also provides the necessary framework for detailed cost estimating and control along with providing guidance for schedule development and control.

a. Work breakdown structure
b. 8.3 filename
c. Back-end database
d. 68-95-99.7 rule

7. The general definition of an _____ is an evaluation of a person, organization, system, process, project or product. _____s are performed to ascertain the validity and reliability of information; also to provide an assessment of a system's internal control. The goal of an _____ is to express an opinion on the person / organization/system (etc) in question, under evaluation based on work done on a test basis.
a. AACR2
b. ACID
c. AACE International
d. Audit

Chapter 8. Scheduling

8. The _____, abbreviated _____ is a mathematically based algorithm for scheduling a set of project activities. It is an important tool for effective project management.

It was developed in the 1950s by the Dupont Corporation at about the same time that General Dynamics and the US Navy were developing the Program Evaluation and Review Technique (PERT) Today, it is commonly used with all forms of projects, including construction, software development, research projects, product development, engineering, and plant maintenance, among others.

   a. Critical path method
   b. 68-95-99.7 rule
   c. Back-end database
   d. 8.3 filename

9. In probability theory and statistics, the _____ is a family of continuous probability distributions defined on the interval [0, 1] parameterized by two positive shape parameters, typically denoted by α and β. It is the special case of the Dirichlet distribution with only two parameters. Since the Dirichlet distribution is the conjugate prior of the multinomial distribution, the _____ is the conjugate prior of the binomial distribution.

   a. Beta distribution
   b. Back-end database
   c. 68-95-99.7 rule
   d. 8.3 filename

10. In probability theory and statistics, _____ is a measure of the variability or dispersion of a population, a data set, or a probability distribution. A low _____ indicates that the data points tend to be very close to the same value (the mean), while high _____ indicates that the data are 'spread out' over a large range of values.

For example, the average height for adult men in the United States is about 70 inches (180 cm), with a _____ of around 3 inches.

   a. Normal distribution
   b. Standard deviation
   c. Confounding
   d. Poisson regression

11. In probability theory and statistics, the _____ of a random variable, probability distribution averaging the squared deviations of its possible values from the expected value (mean.) Whereas the mean is a way to describe the location of a distribution, the _____ is a way to capture its scale or degree of being spread out. The unit of _____ is the square of the unit of the original variable.

a. Test set
b. First-hitting-time models
c. Standard score
d. Variance

12. _____ is a term used in subtly different ways in a number of fields, including philosophy, physics, statistics, economics, finance, insurance, psychology, sociology, engineering, and information science. It applies to predictions of future events, to physical measurements already made, or to the unknown.

In his seminal work Risk, _____, and Profit University of Chicago economist Frank Knight (1921) established the important distinction between risk and _____:

'_____ must be taken in a sense radically distinct from the familiar notion of risk, from which it has never been properly separated....

a. AACR2
b. AACE International
c. ACID
d. Uncertainty

13. _____ is the identification, assessment, and prioritization of risks followed by coordinated and economical application of resources to minimize, monitor, and control the probability and/or impact of unfortunate events.. Risks can come from uncertainty in financial markets, project failures, legal liabilities, credit risk, accidents, natural causes and disasters as well as deliberate attacks from an adversary. Several _____ standards have been developed including the Project Management Institute, the National Institute of Science and Technology, actuarial societies, and ISO standards.
a. Regression toward the mean
b. Stitch Pipeline
c. Signals intelligence
d. Risk Management

14. In probability theory and statistics, the _____ is a continuous probability distribution with lower limit a, mode c and upper limit b.

$$f(x|a,b,c) = \begin{cases} \frac{2(x-a)}{(b-a)(c-a)} & \text{for } a \leq x \leq c \\ \frac{2(b-x)}{(b-a)(b-c)} & \text{for } c \leq x \leq b \\ 0 & \text{otherwise} \end{cases}$$

The distribution simplifies when c = a or c = b. For example, if a = 0, b = 1 and c = 1, then the equations above become:

$$\left.\begin{array}{rcl} f(x) &=& 2x \\ F(x) &=& x^2 \end{array}\right\} \text{ for } 0 \leq x \leq 1$$

$$E(X) = \frac{2}{3}$$

$$\text{Var}(X) = \frac{1}{18}$$

This distribution for a = 0, b = 1 and c = 0.5 is distribution of X = (X_1 + X_2)/2, where X_1, X_2 are two independent random variables with standard uniform distribution.

a. 8.3 filename
b. Back-end database
c. Triangular distribution
d. 68-95-99.7 rule

15. _____, commonly known as GERT, is a network analysis technique used in project management that allows probabilistic treatment of both network logic and activity duration estimated. The technique was first described in 1966 by Dr. Alan B. Pritsker of Purdue University and WW Happ.Compared to other techniques, GERT is an only rarely used scheduling technique. The Project Management Institute discarded GERT in its third edition of PMBOK(2004.)
   a. Concurrent engineering
   b. Graphical evaluation and review technique
   c. Critical Chain
   d. HERMES

16. Graphical Evaluation and Review Technique, commonly known as _____, is a network analysis technique used in project management that allows probabilistic treatment of both network logic and activity duration estimated. The technique was first described in 1966 by Dr. Alan B. Pritsker of Purdue University and WW Happ. Compared to other techniques, _____ is an only rarely used scheduling technique. The Project Management Institute discarded _____ in its third edition of PMBOK (2004.)
   a. Product based planning
   b. Problem domain analysis
   c. Project triangle
   d. GERT

17. The _____ in software engineering is a model of the maturity of the capability of certain business processes. A maturity model can be described as a structured collection of elements that describe certain aspects of maturity in an organization, and aids in the definition and understanding of an organization's processes. The _____ has been superseded by the _____ Integration (Capability Maturity Modell.)
   a. 8.3 filename
   b. Back-end database
   c. 68-95-99.7 rule
   d. Capability Maturity Model

18. _____ is the discipline of planning, organizing and managing resources to bring about the successful completion of specific project goals and objectives.

A project is a finite endeavor--having specific start and completion dates--undertaken to meet particular goals and objectives, usually to bring about beneficial change or added value. This finite characteristic of projects stands in contrast to processes, or operations--which is repetitive, permanent or semi-permanent functional work to produce products or services.

   a. Risk register
   b. SMART
   c. Logical framework approach
   d. Project Management

Chapter 9. Resource Allocation

1. _____ is the calculated approximation of a result which is usable even if input data may be incomplete or uncertain.

In statistics, see _____ theory, estimator.

In mathematics, approximation or _____ typically means finding upper or lower bounds of a quantity that cannot readily be computed precisely and is also an educated guess .

   a. AACR2
   b. AACE International
   c. ACID
   d. Estimation

2. _____ is used to assign the available resources in an economic way. It is part of resource management.

In strategic planning,is a plan for using available resources, for example human resources, especially in the near term, to achieve goals for the future.

   a. Back-end database
   b. 8.3 filename
   c. 68-95-99.7 rule
   d. Resource allocation

3. _____ in project management refers to uncontrolled changes in a project's scope. This phenomenon can occur when the scope of a project is not properly defined, documented, or controlled. It is generally considered a negative occurrence that is to be avoided.
   a. Graphical Evaluation and Review Technique
   b. Problem domain analysis
   c. Student syndrome
   d. Scope creep

4. _____ is the identification, assessment, and prioritization of risks followed by coordinated and economical application of resources to minimize, monitor, and control the probability and/or impact of unfortunate events.. Risks can come from uncertainty in financial markets, project failures, legal liabilities, credit risk, accidents, natural causes and disasters as well as deliberate attacks from an adversary. Several _____ standards have been developed including the Project Management Institute, the National Institute of Science and Technology, actuarial societies, and ISO standards.

a. Risk Management
b. Signals intelligence
c. Regression toward the mean
d. Stitch Pipeline

5. The _____, abbreviated _____ is a mathematically based algorithm for scheduling a set of project activities. It is an important tool for effective project management.

It was developed in the 1950s by the Dupont Corporation at about the same time that General Dynamics and the US Navy were developing the Program Evaluation and Review Technique (PERT) Today, it is commonly used with all forms of projects, including construction, software development, research projects, product development, engineering, and plant maintenance, among others.

a. Critical path method
b. 8.3 filename
c. Back-end database
d. 68-95-99.7 rule

6. _____ is a term that refers both to:

- a formal discipline used to help appraise, or assess, the case for a project or proposal, which itself is a process known as project appraisal; and
- an informal approach to making decisions of any kind.

Under both definitions the process involves, whether explicitly or implicitly, weighing the total expected costs against the total expected benefits of one or more actions in order to choose the best or most profitable option. The formal process is often referred to as either CBA (_____) or BCost-benefit analysis

A hallmark of CBA is that all benefits and all costs are expressed in money terms, and are adjusted for the time value of money, so that all flows of benefits and flows of project costs over time (which tend to occur at different points in time) are expressed on a common basis in terms of their 'present value.' Closely related, but slightly different, formal techniques include Cost-effectiveness analysis, Economic impact analysis, Fiscal impact analysis and Social Return on Investment(SROI) analysis. The latter builds upon the logic of _____, but differs in that it is explicitly designed to inform the practical decision-making of enterprise managers and investors focused on optimising their social and environmental impacts.

Chapter 9. Resource Allocation

a. Groups decision making
b. 68-95-99.7 rule
c. Cost-benefit analysis
d. 8.3 filename

7. _____ is the discipline of planning, organizing and managing resources to bring about the successful completion of specific project goals and objectives.

A project is a finite endeavor--having specific start and completion dates--undertaken to meet particular goals and objectives, usually to bring about beneficial change or added value. This finite characteristic of projects stands in contrast to processes, or operations--which is repetitive, permanent or semi-permanent functional work to produce products or services.

a. SMART
b. Risk register
c. Project management
d. Logical framework approach

8. A _____ is a type of bar chart that illustrates a project schedule. _____s illustrate the start and finish dates of the terminal elements and summary elements of a project. Terminal elements and summary elements comprise the work breakdown structure of the project.
a. 68-95-99.7 rule
b. Back-end database
c. 8.3 filename
d. Gantt chart

9. _____ is a project management process used to examine a project for an unbalanced use of resources (usually people) over time, and for resolving over-allocations or conflicts.

When performing project planning activities, the manager will attempt to schedule certain tasks simultaneously. When more resources such as machines or people are needed than are available, or perhaps a specific person is needed in both tasks, the tasks will have to be rescheduled concurrently or even sequentially to manage the constraint.

a. Project accounting
b. Program management
c. GERT
d. Resource leveling

Chapter 9. Resource Allocation

10. _____ is a term used in subtly different ways in a number of fields, including philosophy, physics, statistics, economics, finance, insurance, psychology, sociology, engineering, and information science. It applies to predictions of future events, to physical measurements already made, or to the unknown.

In his seminal work Risk, _____, and Profit University of Chicago economist Frank Knight (1921) established the important distinction between risk and _____:

'_____ must be taken in a sense radically distinct from the familiar notion of risk, from which it has never been properly separated....

a. AACR2
b. Uncertainty
c. ACID
d. AACE International

11. _____ is an adjective for experience-based techniques that help in problem solving, learning and discovery. A _____ method is particularly used to rapidly come to a solution that is hoped to be close to the best possible answer, or 'optimal solution'. _____s are 'rules of thumb', educated guesses, intuitive judgments or simply common sense.
a. 8.3 filename
b. Partition
c. Heuristic
d. 68-95-99.7 rule

12. _____ is a general algorithm for finding optimal solutions of various optimization problems, especially in discrete and combinatorial optimization. It consists of a systematic enumeration of all candidate solutions, where large subsets of fruitless candidates are discarded en masse, by using upper and lower estimated bounds of the quantity being optimized.

The method was first proposed by A. H. Land and A. G. Doig in 1960 for linear programming.

a. Back-end database
b. 68-95-99.7 rule
c. 8.3 filename
d. Branch and bound

13. _____ is part of project management, which relates to the use of schedules such as Gantt charts to plan and subsequently report progress within the project environment.

Initially, the project scope is defined and the appropriate methods for completing the project are determined. Following this step, the durations for the various tasks necessary to complete the work are listed and grouped into a work breakdown structure.

Chapter 9. Resource Allocation 41

   a. Project planning
   b. Cone of Uncertainty
   c. Project manager
   d. Project plan

14. _____ in organizations and public policy is both the organizational process of creating and maintaining a plan; and the psychological process of thinking about the activities required to create a desired goal on some scale. As such, it is a fundamental property of intelligent behavior. This thought process is essential to the creation and refinement of a plan, or integration of it with other plans, that is, it combines forecasting of developments with the preparation of scenarios of how to react to them.
   a. Planning
   b. 68-95-99.7 rule
   c. Back-end database
   d. 8.3 filename

15. _____ is the mathematical study of waiting lines (or queues.) The theory enables mathematical analysis of several related processes, including arriving at the (back of the) queue, waiting in the queue (essentially a storage process), and being served by the server(s) at the front of the queue. The theory permits the derivation and calculation of several performance measures including the average waiting time in the queue or the system, the expected number waiting or receiving service and the probability of encountering the system in certain states, such as empty, full, having an available server or having to wait a certain time to be served.
   a. Queueing theory
   b. Back-end database
   c. 8.3 filename
   d. 68-95-99.7 rule

16. _____ Project Management (Critical ChainPM) is a method of planning and managing projects that puts the main emphasis on the resources required to execute project tasks. It was developed by Eliyahu M. Goldratt. This is in contrast to the more traditional Critical Path and PERT methods, which emphasize task order and rigid scheduling.
   a. Project team
   b. GERT
   c. Project plan
   d. Critical chain

17. _____ is an overall management philosophy introduced by Dr. Eliyahu M. Goldratt in his 1984 book titled The Goal, that is geared to help organizations continually achieve their goal. The title comes from the contention that any manageable system is limited in achieving more of its goal by a very small number of constraints, and that there is always at least one constraint. The _____ process seeks to identify the constraint and restructure the rest of the organization around it, through the use of the Five Focusing Steps.
   a. Theory of Constraints
   b. Back-end database
   c. 68-95-99.7 rule
   d. 8.3 filename

Chapter 10. Monitoring and Information Systems

1. The _____ in a business or professional enterprise is the department or group that defines and maintains the standards of process, generally related to project management, within the organization. The _____ strives to standardize and introduce economies of repetition in the execution of projects. The _____ is the source of documentation, guidance and metrics on the practice of project management and execution.
   a. Project triangle
   b. Project management office
   c. Nonlinear Management
   d. Commissioning Management Systems

2. _____ is part of project management, which relates to the use of schedules such as Gantt charts to plan and subsequently report progress within the project environment.

Initially, the project scope is defined and the appropriate methods for completing the project are determined. Following this step, the durations for the various tasks necessary to complete the work are listed and grouped into a work breakdown structure.

   a. Project plan
   b. Project manager
   c. Project planning
   d. Cone of Uncertainty

3. _____ is the identification, assessment, and prioritization of risks followed by coordinated and economical application of resources to minimize, monitor, and control the probability and/or impact of unfortunate events.. Risks can come from uncertainty in financial markets, project failures, legal liabilities, credit risk, accidents, natural causes and disasters as well as deliberate attacks from an adversary. Several _____ standards have been developed including the Project Management Institute, the National Institute of Science and Technology, actuarial societies, and ISO standards.
   a. Risk Management
   b. Signals intelligence
   c. Regression toward the mean
   d. Stitch Pipeline

4. _____ in organizations and public policy is both the organizational process of creating and maintaining a plan; and the psychological process of thinking about the activities required to create a desired goal on some scale. As such, it is a fundamental property of intelligent behavior. This thought process is essential to the creation and refinement of a plan, or integration of it with other plans, that is, it combines forecasting of developments with the preparation of scenarios of how to react to them.

Chapter 10. Monitoring and Information Systems

a. Back-end database
b. 68-95-99.7 rule
c. 8.3 filename
d. Planning

5. _____ is the discipline of planning, organizing and managing resources to bring about the successful completion of specific project goals and objectives.

A project is a finite endeavor--having specific start and completion dates--undertaken to meet particular goals and objectives, usually to bring about beneficial change or added value. This finite characteristic of projects stands in contrast to processes, or operations--which is repetitive, permanent or semi-permanent functional work to produce products or services.

a. Risk register
b. Logical framework approach
c. SMART
d. Project management

6. A command center (often called a _____) is any place that is used to provide centralised command for some purpose. While frequently considered to be a military facility, these can be used in many other cases by governments or businesses. The term '_____' is also often used in politics to refer to teams of communications people who monitor and listen to the media and the public, respond to inquiries, and synthesize opinions to determine the best course of action.

a. Salesforce.com
b. Social Return on Investment
c. Report2Web
d. War room

7. _____ is a term used to describe a process of preparing and collecting data - for example as part of a process improvement or similar project. The purpose of _____ is to obtain information to keep on record, to make decisions about important issues, to pass information on to others. Primarily, data is collected to provide information regarding a specific topic .

a. General Social Survey
b. Test method
c. Data collection
d. Public survey

Chapter 10. Monitoring and Information Systems 45

8. Moral psychology is a field of study in both philosophy and psychology. Some use the term 'moral psychology' relatively narrowly to refer to the study of moral development. However, others tend to use the term more broadly to include any topics at the intersection of _____ and psychology (and philosophy of mind.)
    a. AACE International
    b. ACID
    c. Ethics
    d. AACR2

9. A _____ is a professional in the field of project management. _____s can have the responsibility of the planning, execution, and closing of any project, typically relating to construction industry, architecture, computer networking, telecommunications or software development.

Many other fields in the production, design and service industries also have _____s.

   a. Schedule chicken
   b. Project management office
   c. Project manager
   d. Logical framework approach

10. A _____ in project management and systems engineering, is a tool used to define and group a project's discrete work elements (or tasks) in a way that helps organize and define the total work scope of the project.

A _____ element may be a product, data, a service, or any combination. A _____ also provides the necessary framework for detailed cost estimating and control along with providing guidance for schedule development and control.

   a. Back-end database
   b. Work breakdown structure
   c. 68-95-99.7 rule
   d. 8.3 filename

11. _____ in project management is the budgeted cost of work that has actually been performed in carrying out a scheduled task during a specific time period. The term is connected with Earned value management and here it is different from:

   - Budgeted Cost of Work Scheduled (BCWS) : the approved budget that has been allocated to complete a scheduled task during a specific time period.
   - Actual Cost of Work Performed (ACWP) : the actual cost that has been spent, rather than the budgeted cost.

Chapter 10. Monitoring and Information Systems

As example of the difference assume that a schedule contains:

- a task 'Test hardware' that is budgeted to cost $1000 to perform, and
- is expected to begin at the start of January 1 and
- complete at the end of January 10.

At the end of January 5, the work is scheduled to be 50% complete (5 days of the scheduled 10 days.) So, at the end of January 5,

- the BCWS is $1000 (the budgeted cost) times 50% (the scheduled completion percentage) the work is actually only 30% complete. In this case,

    o the BCWP would be $1000 (budgeted cost) times 30% (the actual completion percentage) suppose that to reach the 30% complete level at the end of January 5, $250 was actually spent.

        ■ Then, the ACWP would be $250.

a. Budgeted cost of work performed
b. Student syndrome
c. Mandated Lead Arranger
d. Cone of Uncertainty

12. _____ is the calculated approximation of a result which is usable even if input data may be incomplete or uncertain.

In statistics, see _____ theory, estimator.

In mathematics, approximation or _____ typically means finding upper or lower bounds of a quantity that cannot readily be computed precisely and is also an educated guess .

a. AACE International
b. ACID
c. AACR2
d. Estimation

13. In probability theory and statistics, the _____ of a random variable, probability distribution averaging the squared deviations of its possible values from the expected value (mean.) Whereas the mean is a way to describe the location of a distribution, the _____ is a way to capture its scale or degree of being spread out. The unit of _____ is the square of the unit of the original variable.

Chapter 10. Monitoring and Information Systems 47

a. Variance
b. Standard score
c. Test set
d. First-hitting-time models

14. In a general sense, the term _____ refers to a system of people, data records and activities that process the data and information in an organization, and it includes the organization's manual and automated processes. In a narrow sense, the term _____ refers to the specific application software that is used to store data records in a computer system and automates some of the information-processing activities of the organization. Computer-based _____s are in the field of information technology.
   a. AACE International
   b. AACR2
   c. ACID
   d. Information system

15. A _____ is a subset of the overall internal controls of a business covering the application of people, documents, technologies, and procedures by management accountants to solving business problems such as costing a product, service or a business-wide strategy. _____s are distinct from regular information systems in that they are used to analyze other information systems applied in operational activities in the organization. Academically, the term is commonly used to refer to the group of information management methods tied to the automation or support of human decision making, e.g. Decision Support Systems, Expert systems, and Executive information systems.
   a. RODIN Data Asset Management
   b. Strategic information system
   c. Hierarchical storage management
   d. Management information system

16. A _____ is a type of bar chart that illustrates a project schedule. _____s illustrate the start and finish dates of the terminal elements and summary elements of a project. Terminal elements and summary elements comprise the work breakdown structure of the project.
   a. Back-end database
   b. 68-95-99.7 rule
   c. 8.3 filename
   d. Gantt chart

Chapter 11. Project Control

1. _____ is a term that refers both to:

   - a formal discipline used to help appraise, or assess, the case for a project or proposal, which itself is a process known as project appraisal; and
   - an informal approach to making decisions of any kind.

Under both definitions the process involves, whether explicitly or implicitly, weighing the total expected costs against the total expected benefits of one or more actions in order to choose the best or most profitable option. The formal process is often referred to as either CBA (_____) or BCost-benefit analysis

A hallmark of CBA is that all benefits and all costs are expressed in money terms, and are adjusted for the time value of money, so that all flows of benefits and flows of project costs over time (which tend to occur at different points in time) are expressed on a common basis in terms of their 'present value.' Closely related, but slightly different, formal techniques include Cost-effectiveness analysis, Economic impact analysis, Fiscal impact analysis and Social Return on Investment(SROI) analysis. The latter builds upon the logic of _____, but differs in that it is explicitly designed to inform the practical decision-making of enterprise managers and investors focused on optimising their social and environmental impacts.

   a. 8.3 filename
   b. Cost-benefit analysis
   c. Groups decision making
   d. 68-95-99.7 rule

2. _____ is the discipline of planning, organizing and managing resources to bring about the successful completion of specific project goals and objectives.

A project is a finite endeavor--having specific start and completion dates--undertaken to meet particular goals and objectives, usually to bring about beneficial change or added value. This finite characteristic of projects stands in contrast to processes, or operations--which is repetitive, permanent or semi-permanent functional work to produce products or services.

   a. Logical framework approach
   b. Risk register
   c. SMART
   d. Project management

3. A _____ is a type of bar chart that illustrates a project schedule. _____s illustrate the start and finish dates of the terminal elements and summary elements of a project. Terminal elements and summary elements comprise the work breakdown structure of the project.

Chapter 11. Project Control

a. Back-end database
b. 8.3 filename
c. 68-95-99.7 rule
d. Gantt chart

4. _____ in project management is a tangible or intangible object produced as a result of project execution, as part of an obligation. The term can be either a noun: an item, product or artifact which must be created and then delivered as part of an obligation, or an adjective: describing something which must be delivered as part of an obligation. Like many terms common in corporate usage, the word is considered corporate jargon or corporatese, referring specifically to goals.
   a. 68-95-99.7 rule
   b. Deliverable
   c. Pivot point calculations
   d. Negative volume index

5. _____ in organizations and public policy is both the organizational process of creating and maintaining a plan; and the psychological process of thinking about the activities required to create a desired goal on some scale. As such, it is a fundamental property of intelligent behavior. This thought process is essential to the creation and refinement of a plan, or integration of it with other plans, that is, it combines forecasting of developments with the preparation of scenarios of how to react to them.
   a. 68-95-99.7 rule
   b. 8.3 filename
   c. Planning
   d. Back-end database

6. Moral psychology is a field of study in both philosophy and psychology. Some use the term 'moral psychology' relatively narrowly to refer to the study of moral development. However, others tend to use the term more broadly to include any topics at the intersection of _____ and psychology (and philosophy of mind.)
   a. AACR2
   b. AACE International
   c. ACID
   d. Ethics

7. _____ in project management refers to uncontrolled changes in a project's scope. This phenomenon can occur when the scope of a project is not properly defined, documented, or controlled. It is generally considered a negative occurrence that is to be avoided.

a. Graphical Evaluation and Review Technique
b. Problem domain analysis
c. Scope creep
d. Student syndrome

8. The general definition of an _____ is an evaluation of a person, organization, system, process, project or product. _____s are performed to ascertain the validity and reliability of information; also to provide an assessment of a system's internal control. The goal of an _____ is to express an opinion on the person / organization/system (etc) in question, under evaluation based on work done on a test basis.
   a. AACR2
   b. AACE International
   c. ACID
   d. Audit

9. _____ is the process of comparing the cost, cycle time, productivity, or quality of a specific process or method to another that is widely considered to be an industry standard or best practice. Essentially, _____ provides a snapshot of the performance of your business and helps you understand where you are in relation to a particular standard. The result is often a business case for making changes in order to make improvements.
   a. 8.3 filename
   b. Back-end database
   c. Benchmarking
   d. 68-95-99.7 rule

10. The _____, abbreviated _____ is a mathematically based algorithm for scheduling a set of project activities. It is an important tool for effective project management.

It was developed in the 1950s by the Dupont Corporation at about the same time that General Dynamics and the US Navy were developing the Program Evaluation and Review Technique (PERT) Today, it is commonly used with all forms of projects, including construction, software development, research projects, product development, engineering, and plant maintenance, among others.

   a. 68-95-99.7 rule
   b. 8.3 filename
   c. Critical path method
   d. Back-end database

Chapter 11. Project Control

11. _____ in project management is the budgeted cost of work that has actually been performed in carrying out a scheduled task during a specific time period. The term is connected with Earned value management and here it is different from:

- Budgeted Cost of Work Scheduled (BCWS) : the approved budget that has been allocated to complete a scheduled task during a specific time period.
- Actual Cost of Work Performed (ACWP) : the actual cost that has been spent, rather than the budgeted cost.

As example of the difference assume that a schedule contains:

- a task 'Test hardware' that is budgeted to cost $1000 to perform, and
- is expected to begin at the start of January 1 and
- complete at the end of January 10.

At the end of January 5, the work is scheduled to be 50% complete (5 days of the scheduled 10 days.) So, at the end of January 5,

- the BCWS is $1000 (the budgeted cost) times 50% (the scheduled completion percentage) the work is actually only 30% complete. In this case,
  - the BCWP would be $1000 (budgeted cost) times 30% (the actual completion percentage) suppose that to reach the 30% complete level at the end of January 5, $250 was actually spent.
    - Then, the ACWP would be $250.

a. Student syndrome
b. Mandated Lead Arranger
c. Budgeted cost of work performed
d. Cone of Uncertainty

12. The _____ in a business or professional enterprise is the department or group that defines and maintains the standards of process, generally related to project management, within the organization. The _____ strives to standardize and introduce economies of repetition in the execution of projects. The _____ is the source of documentation, guidance and metrics on the practice of project management and execution.
a. Project triangle
b. Nonlinear Management
c. Commissioning Management Systems
d. Project management office

Chapter 11. Project Control

13. A command center (often called a _____) is any place that is used to provide centralised command for some purpose. While frequently considered to be a military facility, these can be used in many other cases by governments or businesses. The term '_____' is also often used in politics to refer to teams of communications people who monitor and listen to the media and the public, respond to inquiries, and synthesize opinions to determine the best course of action.
    a. Salesforce.com
    b. Social Return on Investment
    c. War room
    d. Report2Web

14. The _____ in software engineering is a model of the maturity of the capability of certain business processes. A maturity model can be described as a structured collection of elements that describe certain aspects of maturity in an organization, and aids in the definition and understanding of an organization's processes. The _____ has been superseded by the _____ Integration (Capability Maturity Modell.)
    a. 8.3 filename
    b. 68-95-99.7 rule
    c. Back-end database
    d. Capability Maturity Model

15. _____ is a family of standards for quality management systems. _____ is maintained by ISO, the International Organization for Standardization and is administered by accreditation and certification bodies. The rules are updated, the time and changes in the requirements for quality, motivate change.
    a. AACE International
    b. ACID
    c. ISO 9000
    d. AACR2

Chapter 12. Project Auditing

1. _____ is a business management strategy, initially implemented by Motorola, that today enjoys widespread application in many sectors of industry.

_____ seeks to improve the quality of process outputs by identifying and removing the causes of defects (errors) and variation in manufacturing and business processes. It uses a set of quality management methods, including statistical methods, and creates a special infrastructure of people within the organization ('Black Belts' etc.)

   a. Back-end database
   b. 8.3 filename
   c. 68-95-99.7 rule
   d. Six Sigma

2. _____ in project management is a tangible or intangible object produced as a result of project execution, as part of an obligation. The term can be either a noun: an item, product or artifact which must be created and then delivered as part of an obligation, or an adjective: describing something which must be delivered as part of an obligation. Like many terms common in corporate usage, the word is considered corporate jargon or corporatese, referring specifically to goals.
   a. Pivot point calculations
   b. 68-95-99.7 rule
   c. Negative volume index
   d. Deliverable

3. _____ is the discipline of planning, organizing and managing resources to bring about the successful completion of specific project goals and objectives.

A project is a finite endeavor--having specific start and completion dates--undertaken to meet particular goals and objectives, usually to bring about beneficial change or added value. This finite characteristic of projects stands in contrast to processes, or operations--which is repetitive, permanent or semi-permanent functional work to produce products or services.

   a. Project management
   b. Logical framework approach
   c. Risk register
   d. SMART

4. The _____ in a business or professional enterprise is the department or group that defines and maintains the standards of process, generally related to project management, within the organization. The _____ strives to standardize and introduce economies of repetition in the execution of projects. The _____ is the source of documentation, guidance and metrics on the practice of project management and execution.

a. Commissioning Management Systems
b. Nonlinear Management
c. Project management office
d. Project triangle

5. A command center (often called a _____) is any place that is used to provide centralised command for some purpose. While frequently considered to be a military facility, these can be used in many other cases by governments or businesses. The term '_____' is also often used in politics to refer to teams of communications people who monitor and listen to the media and the public, respond to inquiries, and synthesize opinions to determine the best course of action.
   a. War room
   b. Report2Web
   c. Social Return on Investment
   d. Salesforce.com

6. The general definition of an _____ is an evaluation of a person, organization, system, process, project or product. _____s are performed to ascertain the validity and reliability of information; also to provide an assessment of a system's internal control. The goal of an _____ is to express an opinion on the person / organization/system (etc) in question, under evaluation based on work done on a test basis.
   a. AACR2
   b. Audit
   c. AACE International
   d. ACID

7. Moral psychology is a field of study in both philosophy and psychology. Some use the term 'moral psychology' relatively narrowly to refer to the study of moral development. However, others tend to use the term more broadly to include any topics at the intersection of _____ and psychology (and philosophy of mind.)
   a. AACE International
   b. AACR2
   c. ACID
   d. Ethics

Chapter 13. Project Termination

1. _____ is the calculated approximation of a result which is usable even if input data may be incomplete or uncertain.

In statistics, see _____ theory, estimator.

In mathematics, approximation or _____ typically means finding upper or lower bounds of a quantity that cannot readily be computed precisely and is also an educated guess .

   a. AACE International
   b. ACID
   c. Estimation
   d. AACR2

2. _____ in project management refers to uncontrolled changes in a project's scope. This phenomenon can occur when the scope of a project is not properly defined, documented, or controlled. It is generally considered a negative occurrence that is to be avoided.
   a. Student syndrome
   b. Graphical Evaluation and Review Technique
   c. Problem domain analysis
   d. Scope creep

3. _____ is the discipline of planning, organizing and managing resources to bring about the successful completion of specific project goals and objectives.

A project is a finite endeavor--having specific start and completion dates--undertaken to meet particular goals and objectives, usually to bring about beneficial change or added value. This finite characteristic of projects stands in contrast to processes, or operations--which is repetitive, permanent or semi-permanent functional work to produce products or services.

   a. Logical framework approach
   b. Risk register
   c. SMART
   d. Project management

4. _____ constitute a class of computer-based information systems including knowledge-based systems that support decision-making activities.

_____ are a specific class of computerized information systems that supports business and organizational decision-making activities. A properly-designed _____ is an interactive software-based system intended to help decision makers compile useful information from raw data, documents, personal knowledge, and/or business models to identify and solve problems and make decisions.

a. Back-end database
b. 68-95-99.7 rule
c. Decision support systems
d. 8.3 filename

5. The _____ is a systematic, interactive forecasting method which relies on a panel of independent experts. The carefully selected experts answer questionnaires in two or more rounds. After each round, a facilitator provides an anonymous summary of the experts' forecasts from the previous round as well as the reasons they provided for their judgments.

a. Delphi method
b. Group decision support systems
c. Service innovation
d. Learning organization

6. A _____ is a professional in the field of project management. _____s can have the responsibility of the planning, execution, and closing of any project, typically relating to construction industry, architecture, computer networking, telecommunications or software development.

Many other fields in the production, design and service industries also have _____s.

a. Schedule chicken
b. Project manager
c. Logical framework approach
d. Project management office

ANSWER KEY

Chapter 1
1. d   2. d   3. d   4. a   5. a   6. c   7. b

Chapter 2
1. b   2. d   3. d   4. d   5. d   6. d   7. d   8. b   9. d   10. d
11. c   12. d   13. d   14. d   15. d   16. b   17. d   18. b   19. d   20. d

Chapter 3
1. d   2. a   3. c   4. b   5. d   6. a   7. d   8. b   9. b   10. d
11. b   12. d   13. a

Chapter 4
1. d   2. d   3. d   4. d   5. a   6. d   7. c   8. d   9. c   10. d

Chapter 5
1. d   2. b   3. b   4. b   5. a   6. b   7. c   8. d   9. b   10. c
11. d   12. b   13. d   14. d   15. d   16. a   17. d

Chapter 6
1. d   2. c   3. b   4. a   5. b   6. d   7. d

Chapter 7
1. d   2. c   3. b   4. b   5. d   6. b   7. d   8. c   9. b   10. d
11. d   12. d   13. d   14. d   15. d   16. d   17. b   18. d

Chapter 8
1. b   2. d   3. d   4. b   5. c   6. a   7. d   8. a   9. a   10. b
11. d   12. d   13. d   14. c   15. b   16. d   17. d   18. d

Chapter 9
1. d   2. d   3. d   4. a   5. a   6. c   7. c   8. d   9. d   10. b
11. c   12. d   13. a   14. a   15. a   16. d   17. a

Chapter 10
1. b   2. c   3. a   4. d   5. d   6. d   7. c   8. c   9. c   10. b
11. a   12. d   13. a   14. d   15. d   16. d

Chapter 11
1. b   2. d   3. d   4. b   5. c   6. d   7. c   8. d   9. c   10. c
11. c   12. d   13. c   14. d   15. c

Chapter 12
1. d   2. d   3. a   4. c   5. a   6. b   7. d

Chapter 13
1. c   2. d   3. d   4. c   5. a   6. b

www.ingramcontent.com/pod-product-compliance
Lightning Source LLC
Chambersburg PA
CBHW080743250426
43671CB00038B/2856